IPHONE 12
USER GUI

The Complete User Manual For Beginner And Senior To Master And Operate The Device Like a Pro

By

Kelvin L. Wilson

Copyright © 2020 Kelvin L. Wilson

Table of Contents

INTRODUCTION
PRICE AND DATE

OF RELEASE FOR IPHONE 12

While the iPhone 12 and iPhone 12 Pro have already launched, the iPhone 12 mini has a release date of November 13 and starts at $ 699 per career; The saved model will cost $ 729. For this price you will get 64 GB of storage. Pre-orders start on November 6, and as with any iPhone device, the mini will sell throughout your big career.

The 128GB version will cost $ 50, priced at $ 749, while the top 256GB version costs $ 849.

IPHONE 12 SIZE AND DESIGN

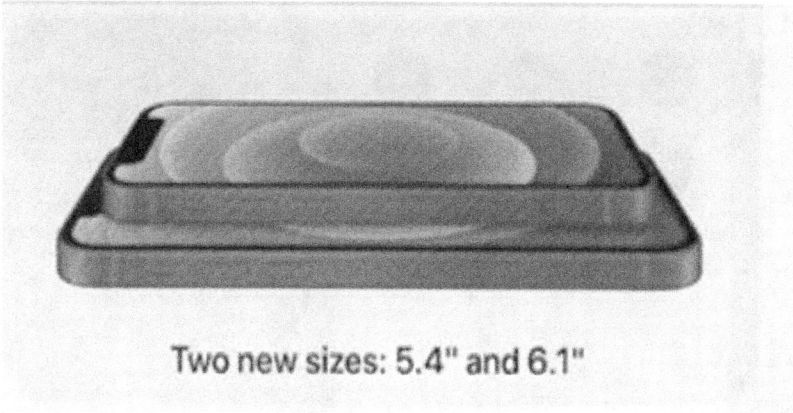

Two new sizes: 5.4" and 6.1"

The iPhone 12 Mini features a thinner left and a flatter frame than the rest of the iPhone 12 line. In some ways, it belonged to the iPhone 5 days ago. The hook unfortunately looks the same size as the previous models.

IPHONE 12 MINI COLORS

The iPhone 12 Mini comes in five colors: black, white, red, red, green and blue. The blue and green colors look and feel fresh on this phone, while the black and white options are for those looking for something more conservative.

DISPLAY AND CERAMIC SCREEN

Apple has incorporated a new type of glass cover for the front of the iPhone 12 Mini, called a ceramic protector. In partnership with Corning, Apple has developed this new technology harder than any other smartphone glass, noting four times better performance performance than existing glass used in iPhones, and the biggest step towards durability even for Apple phones.

Of course, no one can drop the iPhone 12 Mini until it is shipped, but early drop tests on the iPhone 12 and iPhone 12 Pro are promising.

IPhone 12 mini

With the iPhone 12 line, Apple is moving from LCD displays and its cheaper models to Super Retina XDR quality OLED displays. In the case of the iPhone 12 mini, this technology is packaged in a 5.4-inch frame. This makes the footprint of the iPhone 12 Mini significantly smaller than the iPhone SE.

SPECIFICATIONS

It employs the A14 Bionic - the first ever 5nm chip in the phone industry, as well as the rest of the iPhone line. You see 50% faster graphics at Apple's appreciation thanks to its new GPU design, which makes the game look better than ever.

We now need to test the iPhone 12 Mini to get a definite insight into how it works in relation to other phones, including recent iPhones. But our iPhone 12 indices for the A14 Bionic offer big jumps compared to previous models.

CAMERA

Apple spends its first life with seven elements in the iPhone 12 and iPhone 12 Mini, for a significant improvement in performance when shooting in low light conditions. These iPhones also enjoy initial f / 1.6 aperture optics, allowing more light to reach the sensor.

For the first time, all cameras on the iPhone - from the front TrueDepth camera and any rear lens - support night mode. And although the hardware and processing software that supports all of this have been improved, Apple says you can expect much more detail and clarity in medium and low light shooting scenarios since it was possible on iPhone 11 models.

5G

Apple says it's optimizing the entire iOS 14 stack to take advantage of 5G's increased speed. In fact, iOS is set to use only 5G if necessary; If it does not, your iPhone 12 mini will go back to LTE to get the battery life.

Surprisingly, the entire iPhone 12 model, including the mini, supports both 5GHz 5G and 5G millimeter travel.

This means you get the best possible data performance in any country, and downloads of up to 3.5Gbps in urban areas equipped with mmWave buttons.

MINI 12 BATTERY

Apple usually does not release much information about the batteries in their iPhones, so we have to wait for tears before we have heavy numbers on the overall battery capacity of the iPhone 12 mini.

The battery life of the iPhone 12 Mini is 10 hours without streaming video on cable, compared to 11 hours on the larger iPhone 12.

As we suspected, Apple is now packing wireless headphones and charging adapters in the box on all iPhone 12 phones. Cupertino puts this as an initiative out of environmental concerns, but at least it still provides a lightning cable for USB-C in the box.

The iPhone 12 mini is capable of generating 20W wired charging stations, but you need to hop on an optional power adapter for that speed.

MAGSAFE AND CHARGING SPEED

Behind the glass back cover of the iPhone 12 Mini is a new set of MagSafe magnets that helps find the Devic in a wireless charger. These magnets can also be used for new accessories, including an attached wallet and various case designs.

The wireless charging has improved at a record speed of 15 watts which is compatible with Google's pixel phones. We recently tested MagSafe's charging speed on the 6.1-inch iPhone 12 and it reached 32% of the idle in 30 minutes. A 57% drop with the 20-watt USB-C adapter, but we sometimes expect it to be even faster on the iPhone 12 Mini, which packs less battery than any other version of the iPhone 12.

However, iPhone 12 Mini owners should keep in mind that an Apple support document states that the charging speeds of the iPhone 12 Mini with MagSafe will be reduced to 12 watts. We assume it's overheating the little phone.

IPHONE 12 MINIOUTLOOK

The iPhone 12 Mini has the potential to be a big hit, especially if the positive welcome to the standard iPhone 12. The appeal of the iPhone 12 Mini is that it pushes all the major upgrades over the iPhone 11 - even the fastest 5G performance, OLED display A14 Bionic chip faster - In the design of the streamEasy to pocket.

Those who want a bigger screen or a more advanced feature like an Aries camera or a LiDAR sensor are drawn towards the iPhone 12 Pro or iPhone 12 Pro Max. But the iPhone 12 Mini can cause small phones to cool down again. Check out this space as we learn more about the iPhone 12 mini as it comes out this month.

EVERYTHING ABOUT IPHONE 12 MINI

New colors

Two new sizes: 5.4" and 6.1"

New aluminum design

Ceramic Shield

Super Retina

XDR

Dual-camera system

A14

4K

60 fps recording

MagSafe

U1

Water and dust resistant

IP68 6 m

Smart HDR 3

Great battery life

LTE up to 2 Gbps

Face ID

Haptic Touch

CHAPTER ONE

GETTING STARTED

SET UP IPHONE 12 MINI

- Turn on your device
- You must be connected to a Wi-Fi, cellular, or iTunes network to activate and resume your device.
- Tap the Wi-Fi network you want to use or select another option. If you are setting up an iPhone or iPad (Wi-Fi + Cellular), you will need to enter your SIM card first.

Get help if you can't connect to Wi-Fi or if you can't turn on your iPhone.

- Set Face ID or Touch ID and enter an access code

On some devices you can set Face ID or Touch ID. With these features, you can use face recognition or your fingerprint to unlock the device and make purchases. Tap Continue

Next, set up a six-digit password to protect your data. You will need an access code to use features like Face ID, Touch ID and Apple Pay. If you want a four-digit password, a custom password or no password, tap "Password Options".

- Restores or transfers your information and data

If you do not have a backup or other device, select Transfer applications and data.

Sign in with your Apple ID

- Enter your Apple ID and password, or type "Forgot your password or do not have an Apple ID
  When you sign in with your Apple ID, you may be prompted to enter a verification code from your previous device.
- Enable updates automatically and enable other features
- Install Siri and other service

You will then be prompted to configure or enable services and features such as Siri

After signing in follow the steps.

Sets screen time and additional display options

Screen time gives you insights into how much time you and your children spend on your devices. It also allows you to set time limits for daily use of the app.

If you have an iPhone X or later, read more about using gestures to navigate your device. If you have an iPhone 7, iPhone 7 Plus, iPhone 8 or iPhone 8 Plus, you can customize the push of a button on your home screen.

- Click on "Get started" to start using your device

HOW TO TURN OFF IPHONE 12 MINI

How to turn off the iPhone 12 and then restart it

- Hold down the volume and also the side buttons simultaneously for a few seconds.
- Tap the activation icon on the screen at the top of the screen and slide it to the right.

To restart it, long press the side button until the Apple logo appears.

This method performs a graceful shutdown of the iPhone, followed by the standard operating procedure. This is the method you should try to achieve first.

HOW TO FORCE THE IPHONE 12 MINI TO RESTART

- Press and release the volume up button very quickly, followed by the volume up button.

- Press and hold the side button.

- When the Apple logo appears, the sidebar button is released.

While this method tries to restart your iPhone, it may not necessarily solve the problem. Apple's support pages offer additional advice if the iPhone does not turn on again, including how to recover the device in more severe cases.

CHAPTER TWO

APPLE PAY

HOW TO CREATE A NEW APPLE ID

- Launch the settings app.
- Tap Connect on your iPhone at the top of the screen.
- Apple ID shows the steps to enable the settings, then click Sign In
- Tap Do not have an Apple ID or have you forgotten it?
- Click on Create Apple ID.

Apple ID on iPhone Displays the steps Tap Do not Apple ID then tap Create Apple Apple

- Enter date of birth.
- Tap Next.
- Enter your first and last name.
- Tap Next.
- Input your email address or get a new iCloud email address.

Apple ID on iPhone Displays the steps for entering a birthday for the new Apple ID on iPhone

- Enter your email address.

- Create a password.
- Confirm the password.
- Select a security question.
- Type and answer.
- Repeat two more times.
- Enter security questions for a new Apple ID on iPhone
- Agree to the terms.
- Tap Merge.
- Tap Done to confirm.

SETUP GOOGLE MAIL

How to access Google mail, calendar and contacts on iPhone

- Open settings.
- Scroll down and tap Mail.
- Tap Accounts.
- Select Add Account.
- Tap Google.
- Tap Continue when prompted to confirm that Google.com allows you to sign in to your iPhone or iPad.
- Enter your Google Account login information.

Make sure the mail switches, contacts, and calendars in "on" or "off" locations hang where you want them.

- Tap Save.

CHAPTER THREE

APPLE PAY

ADD A CREDIT CARD OR DEBIT CARD

In the wallet, tap the Add Card button.

Do one of the following:

Add a new card or your previous one.

Tap Next and enter the CVV number of each card.

Alternatively, you can attach your card from the bank app or card issuer.

The card changer will determine if your card is eligible for Apple Pay, and may ask you for more information to complete the verification process.

The first card you add to your wallet will be the default payment card. To set another card by default, move it to the front of the stack.

Wallet selects your default card.

Touch and hold the card and then pull it to the front of the stack.

To place another card, touch and hold it and then drag it to a new location.

SEND PAYMENT IN MESSAGES

How do I send payments using Apple Pay Cash

Sending money to friends and family in messages is strangely similar to sending a sticker.

- Open the messages app
- Tap a conversation with the person you want to send money to or start a new iMessage conversation.
- Click on the Apple Pay button.
- Send payments and notifications, show how to open notifications, tap a call and click the Apple Pay button
- Press the - or + buttons to select an amount.
- Tap Show keyboard if you want to enter a specific amount.

Enter your specific amount.

Send payments and notifications, and press the - or + button, then click Show Keyboard and enter your amount

- Tap Pay.

- Press the Submit button (looks like an arrow in a black circle).

Confirm payment by an Apple Pay connected bank card.

Send payments and messages, tap on payment and then tap on send, which is the payment

CHAPTER FOUR

HOW TO SET UP APPLE PAY CASH

First the first thing you need to set up is Apple Pay Cash.

- Open settings.
- Tap Wallet and Apple Pay.
- Tap Apple Pay Cash.
- Tap Continue.

Ask for consent if asked to do so. If you have previously installed Apple Cash on other devices connected to your iCloud account, you may not be prompted to agree

- Tap Done.

VERIFY YOUR IDENTITY FOR APPLE PAY

- Open the settings on your iPhone.
- Tap Wallet and Apple Pay.
- Tap Apple Pay Cash.
- Tap Verified ID.
- Tap Continue.
- Give your first and last name.
- Tap Next.
- Enter your address.

- Tap Next.

HOW TO PUT MONEY IN YOUR APPLE PAY CASH CARD

- Open your iPhone wallet.
- Tap your Apple Pay cash card.
- Tap ... in the black circle in the upper right corner.
- Tap Add money.

Enter the amount of money you would like to add to your card, using the predefined buttons or by entering a custom amount in the number pad.

SEND YOUR APPLE PAY CASH BALANCE TO YOUR BANK ACCOUNT

- Open your iPhone wallet.
- Tap your Apple Pay cash card.
- Tap ... in the black circle in the upper right corner.
- Transfer money to the bank, show how to open the wallet, type Apple Pay Cash Card and click ...
- Tap Transfer to Bank.
- Enter the amount you would like to transfer from your Apple Pay cash balance to your bank account.
- Tap Next.

Choose between direct transfer and 1-3 business days. Please note that direct transfer is taxable and requires a bank card, when choosing 1-3 business days you will need to attach your bank account details.

- Confirm the transfer.

HOW DO I SEND PAYMENTS USING APPLE PAY CASH

Sending money to friends and family in messages is strangely similar to sending a sticker.

- Open messages app
- Tap a conversation with the person you want to send money to or start a new iMessage conversation.
- Click on the Apple Pay button.
- Press the - or + buttons to select an amount.
- Tap Show keyboard if you want to enter a specific amount.
- Enter your specific amount.
- Tap Pay.
- Press the Submit button (looks like an arrow in a black circle).

CLAIM PAYMENT USING APPLE PAY CASH

Of course you can also request payment via messages.

- Open messages on your iPhone.
- Tap a conversation with the person you want to ask for money or start a new iMessage conversation.
- Click on the Apple Pay.
- Press the - or + buttons to select an amount.
- Tap Show keyboard if you want to enter a specific amount.
- Enter your specific amount.
- Tap Request
- Press the Submit button (looks like an arrow in a black circle).

CHAPTER FIVE

DARK MODE

TURN ON DARK MODE

Use night mode on your iPhone

With supported iPhone models, you can use night mode to take pictures when the camera detects an environment in low light.

Take low-light photos with night mode

Night mode will turn on automatically when the camera detects a dim lighting environment. Depending on how dark the scene is, your iPhone may quickly shoot in night mode, or it may take a few seconds. You can also adjust your lighting setting.

For best results, hold the iPhone steady until your finger closes. To pause a night mode image where the photo is completed, simply press the stop button below the slider.

ADJUSTS THE CAPTURE TIME

When shooting in night mode, a number appears next to the night mode icon to indicate how long the shooting lasts.

Then use the slider above the aperture button to select the maximum, which extends the capture time. When you take the picture, Slate sets a timer that will count until the end of the shooting time.

TAKE SELFIES IN NIGHT MODE

- Open the Camera app.

- Press the front camera button.

- Raise and hold your iPhone in your front.

- Take your selfie.

CAPTURE NIGHT TIME VIDEOS

In low light conditions, the night time mode with a tripod can be used to record videos with longer frame rates. Open the camera app and swipe to the left until you see the elapsed time. Tap the Aperture button to shoot your video.

Night mode night time is available on iPhone 12, iPhone 12 mini, iPhone 12 Pro and iPhone 12 Pro Max.

USES A PORTRAIT IN NIGHT MODE

- Open the camera app and slide to portrait mode.

- Follow the on-screen tips.

- Press the aperture button

CHAPTER SIX

SIRI

HOW TO SETUP SIRI

Before taking advantage of the new features released in Siri in iOS 14, you must first verify that Siri is enabled on your iPhone 12.

- Open system.
- Choose Siri & Search.

On the Siri and Search page, make sure the following three options are enabled:

➤ Hear "Hey Siri": This allows you to say the wake-up phrase "Hey Siri" to begin interacting with your voice assistant.

➤ Press Side Button for Siri - This allows you to wake up Siri by long pressing the button on the right side of the phone.

➤ Enable Siri when locked: This allows you to use Siri without unlocking your phone.

HOW TO USE SIRI ON IPHONE 12

Once Siri is enabled on your iPhone 12 to access it, all you have to do is say "Hey Siri" or press and hold the button on the right side of the phone.

With the Siri update in iOS 14, the voice assistant no longer occupies the full screen. Then when you reply, the replies will appear as widgets and banners on one part of your phone screen, but they won't fill the entire screen yet.

CHAPTER SEVEN

HOW TO CHANGE IPHONE 12 MINI LANGUAGE

- ➤ Go to setting
- ➤ Second, open the general part.
- ➤ Then go to the Language and Region tab.
- ➤ Then select the iPhone language and select the preferred language

When selected, press DONE to change the APPLE iPhone 12 mini language

Success! You have just updated your iPhone language!

CHAPTER EIGHT

GET STARTED AND START WITH FAMILY SHARING ON

The family organizer is the person who needs to establish a family partnership first. As a family organizer, you are the one who receives purchase requests, and more importantly, you agree to pay for all the purchases made by everyone in the family group, adult or child.

- Open the Settings app
- Tap the Apple ID banner above.
- Tap the Family Sharing Setup.
- Tap Start.
- Tap Continue. You can attach a photo in advance if you want, but it is not required.
- Tap Continue to share purchases.
- Tap Next to confirm your form of payment.
- Tap Share your location to share it with family or tap Not now.
- Tap Add Family Member and add the person you want to add.

Start typing there.

- Input your credit card security code details when ask

that's it! Just add more friends until everyone in your family joins (up to 6 people). They will receive an email as well as a push notification on their devices asking them to accept your order. If so, all purchases made from that moment will be credited to the family organizer account. And they have instant access to all the others in the group purchases.

HOW TO ACCEPT A FAMILY SHARING INVITATION

- Start settings from the home screen.
- Tap the Apple ID banner above.
- Tap Orders. Should be number 1 next to it (unless you have other orders to wait).
- Tap Accept

Alternatively, you can select a different Apple ID by clicking "on (your name) or using a different ID?"

HOW TO DESIGNATE YOURSELF AS A PARENT OR GUARDIAN

Remember that in order to reach someone as a parent or guardian, you must be the family organizer, that is, the person who builds the family sharing group.

- Open the Settings app
- Tap the Apple ID banner above.
- Tap Family Sharing.
- Tap the person you want to assign as a parent or guardian.
- Tap the switch next to the parent / guardian to turn it on (green is on).

That's it. The same person will now receive purchase requests from all the children in your family sharing group. This means that if one person is busy and cannot approve a request, the other parent can. You still only need one person to receive a request, not both.

CHAPTER NINE

REMINDER

HOW TO CREATE A NEW REMINDER

Start with memories

Create a reminder, add useful details and then mark it as complete when you have done so.

How to create reminder

- Open the Reminders app.
- Tap + New Reminder and enter your reminder.
- Tap Done..

RECEIVE A REMINDER WHEN SENDING MESSAGES TO SOMEONE

Open if you have messages when you want to be notified when you are chatting with a certain person in the messages.

- Open When sending message, tap Select person and then click on a name in your contacts.

The next time you talk to this person, a reminder message will appear.

CHAPTER TEN

CUSTOMIZE XBOX ONE CONTROLLER WITH IPHONE

- Open the settings app.
- Click Bluetooth. Bluetooth may already be there, but if not, the Bluetooth at the top of the next page will turn green.

While the Bluetooth menu is still open, lift your Xbox One controller and make sure it is charged. Make it happen by clicking the Xbox logo button.

- Press and hold the wireless sign-in button on the back of your Xbox One controller for a few seconds. The light on the Xbox button should start flashing quickly (if your Xbox One controller is not yet connected from another device, you can usually skip this step. A long press on the Xbox button will be enough to put it in pairing mode.)

On your iPhone 12 mini you should see the "Xbox Wireless Controller" among other devices in the Bluetooth menu. Click on it.

The light on your Xbox button should stop flashing immediately and stay on.

It have been connected.

PAIR A DUALSHOCK 4 COTROLLER WITH IPHONE 12 MINI

- Open the settings app.
- Click Bluetooth. Bluetooth may already be there, but if not, the Bluetooth at the top of the next page will turn green.

While the Bluetooth menu is still open, lift the DualShock 4 controller and make sure it is charged.

- press and hold the PlayStation button at ones and the share button for a few seconds. The light on the back of your DualShock 4 should start flashing again..

The light on the back of your DualShock 4 should immediately change to a red-pink color. Your DualShock 4 is now optimized.

CHAPTER ELEVEN

HOW TO USE PICTURE-IN-PICTURE MODE

- Open a compatible video application, such as the Apple TV application
- Search for your video content
- Press the power button
- In the upper right corner tap on the image icon in the image

You can move the video box up and down on the screen to find a better viewing position when you are doing other things.

If you find that you want to look back to your full video screen, just click on the image icon in the image in the video - this time it will move to the top left corner.

Note to YouTube: The YouTube app restricts image-by-image to premium subscribers. Users could - for one day - see the PiP content on the YouTube site as a solution, but apparently this gap was closed. Interestingly, the videos embedded in third-party sites still match the feature.

CHAPTER TWELVE

CHANGE WALLPAPER

First, let's learn how to change your iPhone wallpapers using Apple's stock library. In addition, some wallpapers change when you use dark mode.

- Open the settings app
- Scroll down and tap Wallpaper.
- Tap Select New Wallpaper.
- Choose the wallpaper you want to.

➢ Dynamic: This is an image from Apple's photo library with effects that fade and respond to the movement of your device.

➢ Still: This is a still image from Apple's photo library.

➢ Live: These wallpapers create a little animation when you tap and hold your finger.

Select an image to enter preview mode.

In preview mode, you can select to turn the perspective zoom on or off. When you release it, you will see your wallpaper move when you tilt your iPhone.

Choose whether you want this wallpaper for the lock screen, the home screen, or both.

SETUP LIVE PHOTOS AS WALLPAPER FOR LOCK SCREEN

- Go to Settings> Wallpaper.
- Tap Select New Wallpaper. Scroll down and tap on live images.
- Select an image. Make sure you have a live image: Enabled.
- Tap the fence. Select Set Lock Screen or Set Both. Setting the home screen is not critical because the wallpaper does not really move on the home screen.

Once you have done that, you have animated live wallpaper on the lock screen when you tap and hold the image.

ADD A NEW WIDGET TO HOME SCREEN

Add widgets to your home screen

- From the Home screen, touch and hold an applet or an empty area until the apps vibrate.
- Tap the Add Gray button in the upper right corner.
- Select a widget, select from three widget sizes and click Add Widget.
- Tap Done.

You can also add Today's View widgets. From the day view, touch and hold the widget until the quick action menu opens, then click Edit home screen. Drag the widget to the far right of the screen until it appears on the home screen and then tap Done.

EDIT A WIDGET

Modify your widgets

IOS 14 lets you configure your widgets.

Hold the widget and the Quick Actions menu will open then,

- Tap Edit Widget Edit Widget Icon.

Make the changes and click outside the widget to exit.

You can also move your widgets to place your favorites where they are easier to find. Just touch and hold the widget until it giggles and then move the widget to the screen.

ADD WIDGET TO THE TODAY VIEW

- Add widgets to day view
- Touch and hold the widget or empty area in the day view until the apps giggle.

- Tap the Add Gray Plus Icon icon in the top right corner.
- Scroll down to select a widget, then select from three widget sizes.
- Tap Add widget and click Done.

CREATE A SMART STACK

A smart cartridge automatically rotates widgets to display relevant information throughout the day.

- Touch and hold the area on your home screen or day view until the apps giggle.
- Tap the Add Gray Plus Icon icon in the top right corner.
- Scroll down and tap Smart Stack.
- Tap Add widget.

A stack of widgets is displayed on the iPhone

CREATE YOUR OWN STACK OF WIDGETS

- Touch and hold the app or an empty area on the home screen or day view until the apps shake.
- Drag a widget onto another widget.
- Tap Done.

CHANGE WIDGET STACK

- Touch and hold the widget stack.

- Tap to change stack. From here you can reorder the widgets in the stack by dragging the web icon three gray lines. Or millions of users share a widget that is left to delete.

- Tap the gray icon x to remove it when done.

CHAPTER THIRTEEN

SETUP CARPLAY

Connect your iPhone with CarPlay

Set up CarPlay by connecting your iPhone and vehicle to your USB port or wireless feature.

- Make sure Siri is enable on your iPhone
- If Siri is not enabled on your iPhone, go to Settings> Pots and Search, then enable one of the following:
- Press the side button for the pots (on iPhone with Face ID)

CONNECCT WITH USB

Connect your iPhone to your vehicle's USB port using an Apple-approved USB Lightning Cable.

You can mark the USB port with the CarPlay logo or a picture of a smartphone.

CONNECTION WITHOUT CABLE OR WIRELESSLY

- Hold the voice command button
- Your vehicle must be in wireless or Bluetooth pairing mode.

- Go to Settings> General> CarPlay> Cars Available on your iPhone.
- Choose your vehicle.

Note: Some vehicles that support wireless CarPlay allow you to easily connect using your vehicle's iPhone and USB port using a USB lightning cable. If supported after playing CarPlay with USB, you will be asked if you want to adapt Wireless CarPlay for future use. If you agree, the next time you drive, the iPhone will automatically connect to CarPlay.

On some car models, CarPlay Home appears automatically when you connect the iPhone.

If CarPlay Home does not appear, select the CarPlay logo in your vehicle view.

CHAPTER FOURTEEN

TURN VOICE CONTROL

If you are using voice control for the first time, you must configure it by following these steps:

- Start settings from the home screen.
- Tap Accessibility.
- Tap Voice Control.
- Continue tapping "Welcome to Voice Control".
- Tap Next on "What can I say?" screen.
- Set voice control: Tap Continue and then Continue.

TURN ON VOICE CONTROL

If you used voice control before turning it on or off, follow these steps:

- Start settings from the home screen.
- Tap Accessibility.
- Tap Voice Control.
- Tap the on / off control switch. If green is shown, then it has been activated.

CHAPTER FIVTEEN

ADD ANOTHER RINGTONE TO A CONTACT

- Open the Contacts app.
- Select a contact, tap Edit, tap a ringtone and then select a ringtone.
- Turn the ringtone on or off

Turn the ring / silent switch to put the iPhone in ringing mode or silent mode. Clock alarms still ring when the iPhone is in silent mode.

To mute a call, do not interrupt.

HOW TO CHOOSE MESSAGE TONE

Change the default SMS / Text tone

To change the sound you hear for any approaching words:

- Open settings
- Tap a sound
- Tap Text tone
- Select a new sound (Preview of the sound being played as you type)

That's all there's to it. All new text messages activate the new tone when they arrive.

CHANGE THE SMS / TEXT TONE OF A SINGLE CONTACT

- Launch the Contacts app (or the Phone app and select the Contacts tab)
- Tap on their name of the contact you want personalize to open their contact page
- Tap for change
- Tap a tone of text
- Select a new sound

HOW TO SET/CHANGE LANGUAGE

You can change the language setting on iPhone, iPad or iPod touch if it is wrong or if you accidentally changed the language to one that you did not understand.

- Open settings
- Tap General
- On the next screen, tap General.
- Select Language & Region
- Find Language & Region and tap on it.
- Tap Device Language
- Next, tap"Device Language".
- Choose your language
- Select your language from the list.

- Confirm your selection

  Your device will automatically update the language.

HOW TO SET/CHANGE DATE AND TIME

- Settings> General> Date & Time.
- Turn off the device automatically.

You can now change the time zone or the date and time:

- Tap the area zone and enter a city with the time zone you need. Use the time zone map at timeanddate.com to find a city with a time zone that meets your needs.)

Or type the date to change the date and time.

CHAPTER SIXTEEN

MESSAGE APP

SETUP IMESSAGE

How to turn iMessages on or off for iPhone or iPad

If you set up your iPhone with iCloud, chances are iMessage was activated using it. If not, or if you ever need to restart it, it's easy to do!

- Start settings from the home screen.
- Tap Messages.
- You can click on the iMessage on / off switch. When it turn green know it's activated.

SET UP YOUR DEVICE FOR MMS

Set up your mobile phone to MMS

You can send and receive MMS as soon as you log in to your SIM. If this is not the case then maybe your phone can be set up manually for MMS.

- Tap Settings.
- Tap Messages.
- Tap the slider next to "MMS" to turn on the feature.

PIN AND UNPIN MESSAGE

How to Pair Messaging Calls on iPhone with iOS 14

- Go to the messaging app.
  Tap "Edit". In the upper right corner,
- Tap "Edit" in the upper right corner of the messaging app.
- Tap "Edit" in the upper right corner of the messaging app.
- Click "Edit Pins".
- "Edit Pins"from the drop menu..
- Snap messages at the top of the app by tapping the yellow pin icon next to the call.
- Tap the yellow pin icon to catch a call.
- Tap the yellow pin icon to catch a call.
- When done, click "done".

Alternatively, you can pin a call to the top of the app by right-clicking on a call and then tapping "Snap".

You can also press and hold a call and select "Snap" from the drop-down menu.

You can also press and hold a call and select "Snap" from the drop-down menu.

DELETE A MESSAGE

- From the Home screen, tap Messages.
- Tap the message you want want.
- Tap more ...
- Tap the trash icon.
- Tap Delete message.

CHAPTER SEVENTEEN

SETUP MAIL ACCOUNT

If you use an email provider like iCloud, Google or Yahoo, Mail can set up your email account automatically only with your email address and password.

- Go to Settings> Mail, then click Accounts.
- Tap Add account
- Enter your email address and password.
- Tap Next and you will wait to confirm for account.

Select information from your e-mail account, such as contacts or calendars.

- Tap Save.

If you do not see your email provider, tap others to manually add your account.

The iPhone shows how to add a mail account manually

SET UP YOUR EMAIL ACCOUNT MANUALLY

If you do not know them, you can search for them or contact your email provider. Then follow these steps:

- Go to Settings> Mail, then click Accounts.

- Tap Add Account, tap Another, then tap Add Mail Account.
- You need to input your email address, password name, and also the description for your account.
- Tap Next. Mail tries to find your email settings and complete your account creation. When Mail finds your email settings, tap Done to complete your account creation.

DELETE EMAIL ACCOUNT

If you have problems sending and receiving e-mails, you can delete the e-mail account and then create it again.

- Find "Accounts"
- Click on a position.
- Click Mail.
- Click Account.
- Enter the required email account.
- Click Delete Account.
- Click Delete from My iPhone.
- Return to the home screen

RECOVER DELETE EMAILS

Launch the mail app. On the home screen of your iPhone, tap the white envelope icon with the blue background. The mail application interface is loaded on the screen.

Shake your phone. If you accidentally delete an email, just tap your iPhone by hand. A set of pop-ups: "Undo trash?" And "cancel".

Restore Email. Tap "Cancel" and the deleted email will be restored to your inbox.

Note that this only works for deleted emails. If you leave the mail app, you will not be able to retrieve mail.

CHAPTER EIGHTEEN

TAKE A SCREENSHOT ONYOUR DEVICE WITH FACE ID

- Touch and hold the volume up button, and side button.

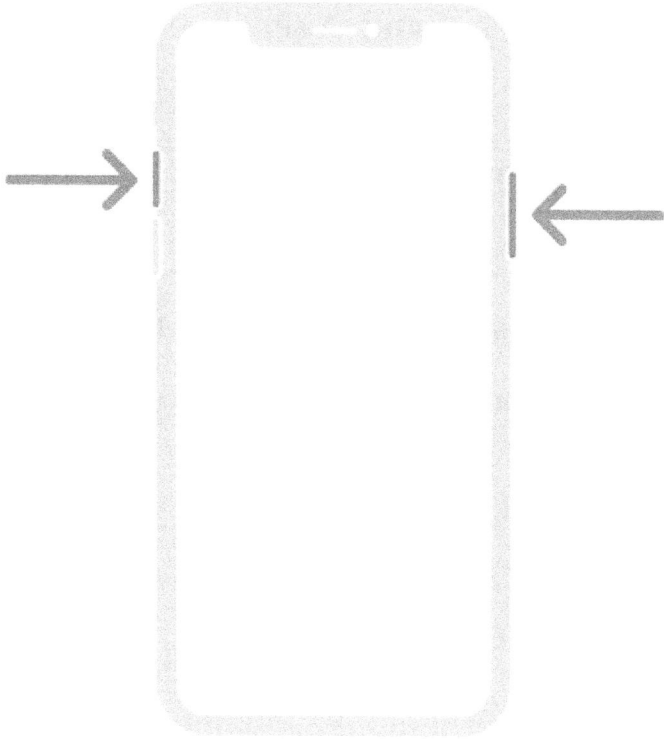

- Release both buttons quickly.

After taking a screenshot, a thumbnail will temporarily appear in the far left corner of the screen. Tap the thumbnail to open it or left click to release it.

HOW TO TAKE A SCREENSHOT OF IPHONE MODELS WITH A TOUCH ID AND SIDE BUTTON

- Touch and hold the home button and the side button.

- Release both buttons quickly.

After taking a screenshot, a thumbnail will temporarily appear in the far left corner of the screen. Tap the thumbnail to open it or left click to release it.

CHAPTER NINTEEN

SET UP THE HEADPHONE LEVEL CHECKER

- Open the settings app.

- Click on Control Center.

- Scroll down and press the green plus (+) button next to Audio.

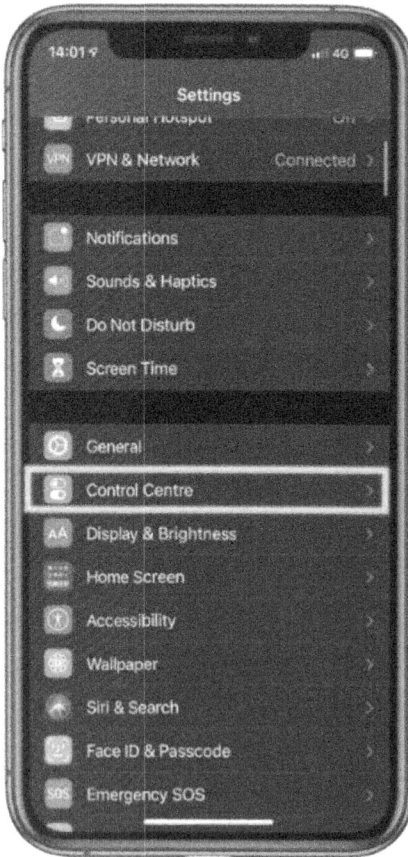

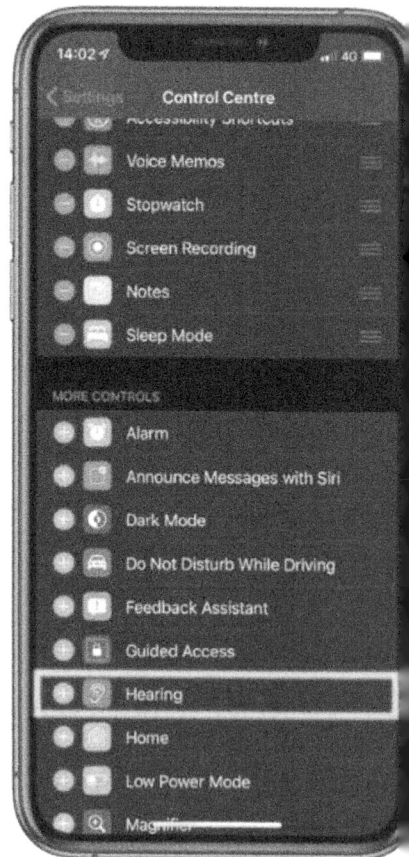

HOW TO USE A HEADPHONE LEVEL TESTER IN IOS 14

The next time you hear something on your iOS device using connected headphones, follow these steps.

- Start control center

In iPad with the Home button, double-click the Home button; On iPhone 8 and above, swipe up from the bottom of the screen; And on iPad Pro 2018 or iPhone X or later, tap from the top right corner of the screen.

- Check the hearing

Aids in the control center. If it has a green mark, listen to a healthy volume level. If what you are listening to is above 80 decibels, the measurement icon will display a yellow exclamation mark, warning you that the volume is too high.

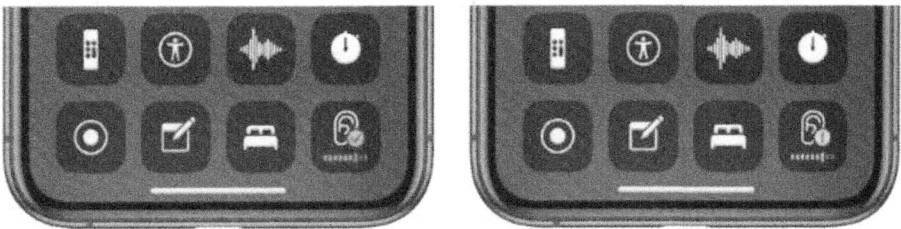

For a more detailed picture of the current decibel level, press the listen button.

Tim's AirPods Pro   100% ▭

Headphone Level
✔ OK   34 dB

■■■■■■■■■■■■■|■■■■■

20   80   110

Live Listen
Off

USE APPLE'S LIVE LIST FEATURE
WITH AIRPODS

The real-time headphone-level feature works well with most headphones, but keep in mind that Apple says the measurement is more accurate with AirPods and other Apple-approved headphones.

CHAPTER TWENTY

SET A SLEEP SCHEDULE ON IPHONE

- Open the Health app.
- Tap the Browse tab in the lower right corner of the screen.
- Scroll down and select Sleep.
- Tap on the sleep schedule under "Your Schedule".
- When the sleep program is off, press the button to switch to the green ON mode.
- Under "Full schedule", type your first schedule.
- Tap on one of the blue circles in the "Active Days" section to turn off the sleep panel any day of the week.
- Using your finger, pull the edge of the sleeping pad to extend it around the clock graph. It defines your sleep progress as well as your bedtime and wake time.
- Scroll down to find out your alarm options. Use the switch next to the wake-up alarm to turn the alarm on / off. Once you have activated the alarm, you can select the type of vibration and sound you want to hear using Sounds & Haptics, adjust the volume

using the slider and enable snooze using the snooze switch.

- Tap Add in the top right corner when done.
- To add an additional schedule for different days (for example, on weekends), type a schedule for other days and customize your options as described in the previous steps.

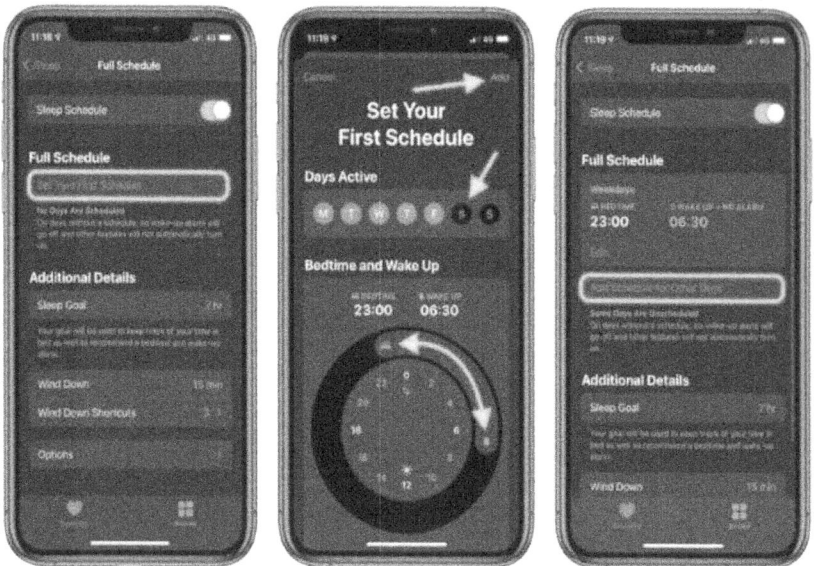

Note that if this is the first time you are setting a sleep schedule after opening the health app and navigating to the sleep section, you will need to tap "Start work" and set a sleep destination before you can set the sleep and adjust the schedule.

CHAPTER TWENTYY ONE

MANAGE APPLICATIONS AND DATA

INSTALL APPS FROM THE APP STORE

Once you have searched for the app you are looking for, it is time to download and install it.

- Tap the app or game you want to buy or download for free.
- Tap Get when it's free, or the price of the app when it's paid.
- Move your finger on the Home Button to activate a Touch ID or double-click the Face ID side button.

HOW TO DELETE APPS

Similar to switching to "past mode" on devices with a three-dimensional touch in the past, the key is to place your finger on an app (no need to press down hard) for a second.

- Look for the app you don't need or would like to uninstall on the device home screen.
- Press and hold the app
- Tap Delete app when menu options appear.

HOW TO DELETE MULTIPLE APPS

Missing the good old days of "juggling mode" on your home screen? It's still there.

Select an app on your home screen (no matter which one you choose).

- Press and hold the app icon for two seconds.
- Tap the X in the top right corner of any app icon you want to remove.
- Tap Finish in the top right corner of your iPhone (or click the Home button on iPhones with one) when done.

CHAPTER TWENTY TWO

LOCATION SERVICES

ENABLE LOCATION SERVICES

How to activate location on iPhone 12

Tasks

Activating location is very useful and essential for using maps in various apps like Uber.

We'll show you how to manage and configure location settings on your iPhone 12 so you can enjoy the benefits of location services.

- Go to Home screen settings.
- Select Privacy.
- Click Location Services and turn on the feature.

Now the applications that need to know your location will send you an alert requesting your access permission

- o Never
- o Ask next time
- o While using the app
- o All the time

Congratulations, you have now activated location on your iPhone 12.

Made in United States
Orlando, FL
05 June 2025